Principles of Fearless Leadership

UNDERSTANDING AND ADOPTING THE

PRINCIPLES OF POWERFUL LEADERSHIP

AND IMPLEMENTING THEM

IN YOUR LIFE

IN YOUR ORGANIZATION

IN YOUR HOME

Oprah,
Thank you so
much for dedicating
your life to making the world
a better place.
Joseph

By Dr. Joseph Gulino

with Nathan Levy and Scott Hobson

Illustrations by Shari Bullard

Nathan Levy Books, LLC

18 Moorland Blvd.

Monroe Township, NJ 08831

Phone: 732-605-1643

Fax: 732-656-7822

www.storieswithholes.com

ISBN 9780984028726

Introduction

• Everyone is a leader at some time in his or her career. A leader can be anyone who has goals to accomplish and who works with others. A leader is NOT just a person with a title.

Are individuals born leaders?

Can individuals learn to become leaders?

Is leadership an art form, is it innate, or is it a skill to be developed?

You can be proactive in developing leadership skills. There is no need to learn from your mistakes.

What are the essential criteria or characteristics that distinguish effective fearless leaders?

Understanding and adopting the principles of fearless leaders and implementing them in your life will establish you or reinforce you as an Effective Fearless Leader.

Special thanks to Martin Kelly.

Acknowledgements from Dr. Gulino's graduate students:

Curriculum Leadership is one of the best and most useful classes that I have taken. With all of the leadership classes, forums, etc. that we took at West Point, I think that this one was more beneficial. We touched on so many real topics that are experienced every day. The biggest strategy that I will take from this class is remaining calm in a debate on issues and not letting emotions get in the way of identifying facts and finding a solution. The knowledge and skills from this course have helped me to be more patient with students and colleagues. I also think that I am going to try to be more selective about picking my battles and focusing on the ones that I think I can win, as opposed to the ones that just need to be brought to the floor for attention, rather than trying to fight them all. I will continue to read about great leaders and their ideas.

- Bill Tharp

....

Dr. Gulino's *Curriculum Leadership* class gave me insights into Leadership issues, administrative structure, and the "Whys" behind the "Whats" that take place in management positions and decision making. Dr. Gulino's observations and insights in the weekly lessons were invaluable. Never have I had the privilege of communication with and guidance from an individual so well-versed in leadership structure. The readings, content, discussions, and responses truly gave me new understandings and perspectives into others and myself as leader. There was so much that I learned from this course from all those who participated. This class has opened my eyes to many other ways of reaching my students and being a leader in my school. I feel more confident with stating my opinion on certain focal points in my school, and I look at everything in a more positive light.

- Leisel Holland

The most useful ideas that I learned in *Curriculum Leadership* course came from the Powell book and from Dr. Gulino's "Pearls of Wisdom." Such as that from a post in one of the most recent threads – something to the effect of "A child is not a grade – a grade is no more than a reflection of what has or has not taken place in the last nine weeks." That seemingly simple statement was a wonderful eye-opener for me. I hear SO much of "My child is an 'A' student," and I never knew how to tell a parent what a stupid statement that was. I am also going to keep Dr. Gulino's notes in the assignments folders. I found them very personal and inspirational. Dr. Gulino, you are very much an inspiration!

- Kimberly Thompson Abarr

....

The structure of *Curriculum Leadership* reflected a very craftsman-like approach. I truly appreciated the carefully-nuanced references and ancillary nuggets of wisdom that were placed in the lessons. The course came at a very key time, and made me look very deeply at some core beliefs I had regarding my workplace and co-workers. This was a good thing. I have done much reflecting on the instructor's and fellow students' comments, and as a consequence, have radically shifted major points of view. I expect this year to be one of the most productive and enjoyable in my career. The course evaluation was glowing. The course was enriching, stimulating, and challenging.

- John MacMurray

....

At this point I feel that I am still digesting what I have learned over this semester. Every day I find opportunities to use some of the knowledge I have gained. I feel very positive about my experiences in *Curriculum Leadership*; and I feel, with time, I will continue to reflect and evolve in my teaching and leadership skills. With this growth, I expect more questions to pop up; but at this point, I am just enjoying my renewed sense of vision and the feeling of power over my own school destiny. I really enjoyed this class. Thank you for your excellent leadership – you truly lead by example.

- Melissa Bierman

Table of Contents

"Write people's accomplishments in stone and their faults in sand."

- Benjamin Franklin

Effective fearless leaders have great self-respect and inner strength. They also respect others enough to forget the problems of the past. They focus on the improvements occurring in the present.

No one is perfect. No one is free of oversight or mistakes in judgment, especially when it is due to a lack of knowledge that they might need to perform effectively. As long as the leader knows that intentions are worthy, faults can be improved upon, corrected, or removed.

Effective leaders focus on growth and improvement. They do not dwell on failures.

Be a seeker
of the 'bulbs.'

Effective fearless leaders take great joy and pride in seeing the 'light bulbs' go on when members of the organization grasp concepts that they may not have understood at an earlier time.

The energy used to turn on those internal bulbs comes from strong and positive leadership (the organization's generator) and ignites knowledge in others which helps move the organization toward greater successes.

Promote freedom
of expression.

Effective fearless leaders never tolerate an environment that prevents the sprouting of great ideas. Therefore, they promote freedom of expression.

They expect that everyone in the organization will be accepting of and accommodating to others.

Effective leaders also expect that every member of the organization will respect others, as they encourage open discussion. They want everyone to share ideas and opinions for the good of the organization.

Leaders model this behavior by accepting all ideas for what they are – ideas. They do not negate anyone's initial proposals or comments.

Be responsible to the persons to whom you answer.

Effective fearless leaders address the needs of their superiors quickly.

They turn in assignments or requests in a timely manner ahead of all due dates. They do not need to be reminded, as they make the needs of their superiors top priority.

Effective leaders understand that how they treat others is how those whom they lead will support them.

They help make their superiors look better and be more successful.

Dazzle them with your footwork.

Effective fearless leaders know that there are times when they need to stage unexpected surprises, attention getters, or stimulating measures or activities. Nothing is worse than working in a lackluster or humdrum environment.

Members of an organization who appreciate their leaders enjoy observing them being successful. They take pride in their leaders' accomplishments.

Effective leaders know it is beneficial to lighten up the days for others in some way. It is normally greatly appreciated and enjoyed; and it strengthens the organization.

Decrease the importance of the yearly summative evaluation.

Effective fearless leaders never sit down at the end of the year and fill out a summative evaluation about another person without prior data documented and communicated previously to the person reviewed.

The summative evaluation should merely be a collection of all that has been discussed or reviewed throughout the year. Comments or concerns that have not been shared earlier in the year should not be included in any summative.

Effective leaders do unto others as they would have others do unto them.

If you fly
by the seat
of your pants,
be prepared for
rocky landings.

Effective fearless leaders use and think through thoughtful researched data before they make any decisions or take any action. They collect information which is tangible, observable, and measurable.

They do not take quick or 'knee jerk' action just because they feel that they should. They make no decisions without taking the time to have all of the facts because they know that making decisions without the facts can lead to hard times and the need to backtrack with 'egg on their face.'

Subjective information can be used in the decision-making process, but only after the hard data is collected and evaluated.

"… Build the team, grow the company, and have fun. Nine words that say it all. A big part of what I do is just love them, work with them on their personal lives and help them understand the basic truths about life."

- Clyde Lear,
Learfield Communications

Clyde Lear.

Principles of Fearless Leaders

Effective fearless leaders know that they are responsible for managing their workplace. They also know that they need to work at building better lives for those whom they lead.

This is important because work life is affected by home life. Happy, centered individuals are more creative, productive, and self-motivated.

Effective leaders know that when they look to the well-being of all, and give of themselves to others to help them meet their needs, a happier staff and a stronger and more successful organization is developed.

If every person you have ever led had the true option to work with you –
to choose you as their leader again –
would they decide to do so?

Effective fearless leaders want the answer to be "YES!"

Individuals who work with effective leaders always say "Yes!" They understand through the experiences of their relationships that their leader cares for them as individuals.

Effective leaders provide everyone in the organization all of the necessary training and tools to achieve goals and personal milestones.

Adapt or be prepared
to fall behind
and fail.

Effective fearless leaders understand the world in which we live is ever-changing and will continue to change at a rapid pace.

They model how to work through change by continually updating themselves and never express negative comments in words or actions when called upon to adapt or change.

Effective leaders also expect and help everyone in the organization to continue to grow and improve by providing them with researched data, current publications, and in-service training opportunities.

Every person, group, division, or echelon of individuals in the workplace must respect and appreciate the work of others.

Effective fearless leaders know that they must model 'respect for all' through their words and actions.

They openly and often recognize the importance of each person or group to the entire organization. When one person or group improves, everybody improves.

Effective leaders know that cooperation between members of the organization must be reinforced. All members of the organization, from those with the greatest amount of responsibility to those at the entry level, must be valued and respected.

Help others learn to organize and develop positive workplace behaviors.

Effective fearless leaders do not just say, "You need to get organized."

They make sure that everyone in the organization knows and understands how to execute the behaviors necessary to complete successful work.

Effective leaders know that it is not important how a desk looks, but how the person behind that desk accomplishes the tasks and responsibilities of her/his position.

They also speak specifically to an individual's area of growth, so that no one has to guess what their expectations might be.

There is no place for whining in your organization, especially on your part.

Effective fearless leaders know that whining is unacceptable. It cannot be tolerated. Its negative effects spread like a cancer throughout the organization.

Most members of the organization will know of the whiner/complainer and that person will lose the respect of peers.

It is very important for effective leaders to have a trusted and positive group of team members with whom they can share, reflect, and count upon.

All leaders must understand how to handle the 'uns'.

Judge

Effective fearless leaders know that when a member of their organization does something that is…

> Unhealthy,
> Unethical,
> Unsafe, or
> Unfair,

…they must confront that member immediately. They must also weigh the negative action in relation to the effects on the organization and act accordingly – remediation or removal.

Effective leaders know that the offending member of the organization is in need of direction or is removing himself or herself from the organization because of their actions.

It takes a team of skilled and cooperative players to achieve a mutual goal.

Effective fearless leaders recognize that groups of individuals in an organization must be prepared and trained to work in teams.

They do not expect that individuals will work cooperatively just because they are teamed together and the leader wants them to work cooperatively.

Effective leaders build the skill sets of the members of their organization. They know that all individuals must earn the opportunities to work cooperatively in teams, gradually and over time.

When prepared, the individuals can be positioned together as teams that will be successful.

We must
know each other
to know each other.

Effective fearless leaders know that they must get to know and understand the individuals with whom they work. They learn to know how each person approaches responsibilities, how they react to new projects and experiences, and how they interact with their peers. They set a time, on a weekly or monthly basis, to meet one-on-one with every individual in their charge.

They work to understand the personal characteristics of everyone in the organization. Are they individuals who see the glass half-full or half-empty? Are they 'brainstormers' or 'processors'? Do they compartmentalize or do they think outside of the box?

Effective leaders are able to take individuals from where they are and encourage them to move forward to where they are capable of going for the good of the individual and the good of the organization.

Find the balance between introducing and reinforcing the fixed set of information that everyone needs to have in order to achieve their greatest potential.

Effective fearless leaders provide meaningful information or learning experiences that actively and emotionally engage those whom they lead.

They understand the timeliness of when to introduce new information and when it is time to reinforce that which has been previously introduced.

Members of the organization are then more likely to absorb and relate to the information in order to apply it when they interact with real-world situations.

This will lead to program or project successes and personal achievements and growth for the individuals and the organization.

Because
I said so!

Effective fearless leaders know that this statement does not guarantee results.

It can possibly be used in the case of an emergency or in times of need for immediate action. However, even then, the leader should try to avoid expressing these words.

Effective leaders, who have worked at gaining the respect of members of their organization rather than power over them, will be followed without having to voice this exclamation.

Positive reinforcement, when well-deserved is a 'no-brainer.'

Effective fearless leaders bring people together to solve problems; and know that when the problems are solved, there are opportunities for positive, public reinforcement.

1. Public reinforcement is not something you need to plan or budget.
2. You do not need to gain permission from anyone to give it.
3. People love to receive public positive reinforcement when it is given appropriately.

"This is the value of the teacher,
who looks at a face and says
there's something behind that and
I want to reach that person,
I want to influence that person,
I want to encourage that person,
I want to enrich, I want to
call out that person
who is behind that face,
behind that color,
behind that language,
behind that tradition,
behind that culture.
I believe you can do it.
I know it was done for me."

- Maya Angelou

Effective fearless leaders live Maya Angelou's remarks through their words and actions. They reach out to individuals with whom they work and help them become better.

Effective leaders look for the good in everyone in their organization and make it a point to connect with them in some way.

They know that their leadership position allows them to challenge each individual to rise to great expectations.

Members of the organization learn to believe they can, because the leader believes they can.

Criticism should be short, to the point, and clear regarding behaviors that should be improved upon or stopped.

Effective fearless leaders know that there is no such practice as constructive criticism. Criticism is criticism. The resonance of the word is negative as it is heard. Using words like assess, review, measure, etc., is more productive.

If at all possible, comments should be made to members of the organization to improve performance, not point out faults.

Effective leaders understand that positive comments to others should not be expressed until there is a valid reason to state them. Positive comments should never be used to ease the pain of poor performance.

Measurement alone does not modify behavior.

Effective fearless leaders know that an efficient system of measurement will allow them to note even minor changes in an individual's behavior. They also know that merely presenting findings to others in paper or electronic form is not the end all of measurement.

They know that they must use the measured data to give feedback and positive reinforcement. Expressing it personally and with sincerity can bring out the best in others.

Effective leaders use the data for positive reinforcement to improve or change behaviors. They do not use negative consequences as their first reaction to behaviors they deem 'need improvement.'

Negative reinforcement produces negative talk and more.

Effective fearless leaders know that all things negative are to be avoided as much as possible.

Though there may be proper times and reasons for negative reinforcement; unless it is an emergency, it should never be in the public eye.

Effective leaders use positive reinforcement such as:

"Go for it,"

"You can do it," and

"Give it a try."

They are only human.

Effective fearless leaders know that everyone has 'off days' and that mistakes will happen. All members of the organization, as well as their leaders, are only human.

When mistakes do happen, effective leaders encourage the members of the organization to acknowledge their errors rather than ignore, avoid, or refuse to address them. A bad situation can only get worse when avoided or not resolved.

Effective leaders know that everyone is not great all of the time and that life's continuum is really about each person's intentions.

Peer reinforcement is important.

Effective fearless leaders believe strongly that all persons in the organization must learn to reinforce and praise others as a duty of their position.

Everyone in the organization must learn how to positively reinforce others through the leader's example. Then, they need to provide that appropriate positive reinforcement to each other.

Effective leaders know that when peers recognize that they can and should praise others, improvement occurs more frequently, much faster, and lasts longer. Instant karma!

There are no 'buts' about it.

Effective fearless leaders know that any comments that start out with praise and then include the word 'but' can never be considered a form of positive reinforcement.

These leaders have conversations with individuals that are singular in purpose and to the point.

Effective leaders never mix the positives with 'constructive criticism' because no criticism is constructive. This approach is certain to leave mixed messages.

"Take time to be silent, to quiet the internal dialogue, to be guided by your intuition, rather than external imposed interpretations of what is good and not good."

- Deepak Chopra, M.D.

Effective fearless leaders know that there are times when they must take time to stop and just be.

There are times to stop actively thinking and leave the mind open to the senses. Ineffective leaders think that they need to always take immediate action to solve problems as quickly as possible.

Effective leaders know that good decisions evolve from timely but deliberate gathering of data (asking the right questions), careful consideration of all of the possible consequences, and then the time to just be.

They only add their gut feelings and move forward when they have all of the data and have had quiet time to carefully process all of that data.

Prepare others to work and live in the future, not only in the present, and definitely not in the past.

Effective fearless leaders understand the importance of reveling in and maintaining the history and traditions of the past.

They know that they must use the past as a bridge to the present and to the future.

Effective leaders reach to the sky for new adventures in improvement, knowing that an organization that is staying still, enjoying the status quo, is really an organization that is moving backward.

They know that development and growth must be constants.

Know how things work, not just that they work.

Effective fearless leaders understand that if they do not know how something works, they may not know whom to call or direct to repair it when things go wrong.

A change in the environment may be the reason why something needs to be repaired or retooled.

Effective leaders understand that they do not always need to know where all the nuts and bolts go to maintain something, but they do know how or why it works well enough to know who to call to repair it.

Pessimists

Curse at the wind

Optimists

Hope for wind to come up

Realists

Adjust the sails

Effective fearless leaders are realists. They waste no time or energy on condemning any of the forces that hinder progress.

They also do not pass off difficulties with a 'pie in the sky' attitude or comments to others that cover up reality.

Effective fearless leaders take stock of negative situations, devise plans with help from others in the organization, retool, and then move forward with a positive attitude.

Engage all individuals in reflective and responsive thinking.

Effective fearless leaders know that they must challenge everyone to be reflective thinkers.

In reviewing and analyzing all situations with others, they promote common values in their organizations, ethical behavior, high ideals and expectations, and principled responses.

Effective leaders know that when the majority of individuals in their organization are reflective thinkers, the organization experiences smoother operation and greater successes.

Listen, listen, listen …
then think …
before you respond.

Effective fearless leaders slow down conversations constructively. Unhurried, deliberate, and thoughtful communication creates positive, cooperative discussions.

Quick conversations, especially in passing, lead to miscommunication and problems due to the lack of careful processing.

Effective leaders listen, listen, listen.... They respect the thought process of the other person speaking. They think before they respond and are sure to acknowledge what they heard and understood. Only then do they state their perspective or response.

Accept responsibility for performance outcomes of others in your charge.

Effective fearless leaders know that their work is not completed by just providing good direction. They know that they are responsible for the results, as well.

It is important to trust that all members of the organization will carry out important tasks properly. It is equally important for the leader to be aware of the intentions and actions of those members.

Effective leaders know that they must have a line of communication that is continually connected, open, honest, and expected, especially when someone lacks experience or is new to the organization.

"The purpose of goal setting should be to increase opportunities for positive reinforcement."

- Aubrey Daniels

Effective fearless leaders understand that the more goals an organization pursues, greater are the number of opportunities for positive reinforcement. Many of these goals can be those of members of the organization if the members are allowed freedom of expression.

The goals of the members are often the same as the leader. As everyone in the organization works toward the many achievable goals, they all reinforce each other positively at every opportunity.

Effective leaders publicly praise members of the organization as often as possible. The leader's ego (or rather, lack thereof) allows others to shine.

Is it a motivation problem or a skill problem?

Effective fearless leaders are skilled at analyzing the behaviors of the members of their organization and can assess when and why something is not right:

1. Is it a problem with a staff member's motivation, or
2. Does the staff member lack the skill, knowledge, or ability to handle the task?

Effective leaders know how to respond to the needs of the members of the organization when they have the answer to that question.

Ineffective practices or people have a long-term negative influence on an organization.

Effective fearless leaders understand that there are consequences to the organization when individuals with poor work ethic or negative behaviors are not addressed. They can choose to help remediate or remove those individuals.

It is most important to never sweep any situation under the rug or avoid communicating mistakes. The problem or concern never goes away or improves by hoping it will do so.

Effective leaders tackle personnel problems head on with compassion, but also keep the need for organizational steady-state as the focus. The organization is never to be sacrificed for any one person.

All people
with whom you work
should regularly receive
proper consequences,
either positive or negative.

Effective fearless leaders plan timely visits (some means of communication) with everyone in the organization, daily, weekly, or monthly.

They know that immediate positive or corrective reinforcement is far more effective than delayed rewards or corrective comments. Delayed communication promotes a sense of uncertainty that muddles effective production and growth.

Effective leaders share valid and meaningful comments to others when they are spot on, doing well, exceeding expectations, or need to improve in an area. And, they do it in a timely manner.

Use everyday action research.

Effective fearless leaders understand that before moving on to a new task or venture, they must be sure that the current one is complete by asking themselves:

1. Did it accomplish what I intended?
2. Do I need to change something due to the results?
3. What would have been the outcome if I had just left it alone?

When effective leaders answer these questions, they are acting upon everything they do and completing tasks by simple reflection.

It can get much more complicated than this for deeper and complex issues, but this is simple everyday action research. When all individuals in an organization are thinking through reflection, the organization experiences smoother operations and greater successes.

Organize to the max and plan ahead – especially when addressing your group.

Effective fearless leaders address the members of their organization creatively. They do not hold a meeting without having good reason for it.

Why do others want to listen to or learn what is being communicated or presented? What is in it for them?

Effective leaders know these are the questions that they should ask themselves as they prepare to speak to any group. No meeting is too short and no group too small to neglect this practice.

If there is no clear reason to address an issue, then why address it?

Being well-prepared helps you expect the unexpected.

Effective fearless leaders know that being well-prepared allows them to handle challenging situations as if they were planned.

New leaders, after experiencing all of the many events, programs, meetings, groups, tasks, etc., for the first time, take stock of everything. They revisit every interaction that they experienced, reflect upon how each was handled, and then plan for how they will handle each one in the future.

Effective leaders take the time to think through how they will manage variables that may be presented to them in the future.

Solve your problems
step by step.

Principles of Fearless Leaders

Problem solving steps of effective
fearless leaders:

1. Define desired results – then
   identify behaviors that will support
   them.
2. Design and administer tools of
   measurement of those behaviors.
3. Shape positive consequences
   of reinforcement that are
   appreciated by others.
4. Provide feedback regarding the
   results to all.
5. Reevaluate the entire
   progression.

Time is important, so if you do not
see improvement or the problem
solved after a designated amount of
time, re-examine the entire process.

Leaders of complex organizations should be able to engage in more than one action or activity at a time.

Effective fearless leaders must learn to develop and use internal radar to continually assess their environments.

They know they must learn to use all of their senses, and often have their senses working at the same time while being involved in more than one activity.

Effective leaders also know it is most important that when they are out and about in the workplace, they use all of their senses to take in data and information.

Using the collected data, they know that it is important to focus one-on-one with individuals to make sure that they experience quality communication.

Do not wait too long before dealing with poor performance.

Effective fearless leaders know to speak up as soon as possible. Hesitation in noting or reinforcing areas for improvement can decrease positive feelings about the person involved to a greater degree than if the leader spoke up right away; and the negative feelings increase over time.

When a leader waits too long to correct a member of the organization, it may be difficult to give honest praise to the minor changes that the other person finally makes or attempts to make.

Effective leaders know that to avoid only delays the inevitable. Problems become more difficult to resolve than when first experienced.

Make your expectations clear.

Effective fearless leaders know that performance expectations must be known and understood by the individuals in their organization. There is no room for confusion.

They also understand that as individuals meet performance expectations, more freedom and personal control can be granted.

With greater freedom comes autonomy, personally-solicited feedback by the organization members, opportunities for positive reinforcement, and growth in leadership potential.

The more goals that are reached, the more opportunities there are to celebrate successes and enhance the work environment.

Be flexible
so you can roll
with the punches
and keep yourself
in a steady state.

Effective fearless leaders are agile. They know that others are paying attention to how they react to all situations. They roll with the punches and do not sweat the small stuff.

They handle the big stuff with calmness and grace. They are able to do this because they stay well-prepared for the obvious and have only good intentions when the surprises arise.

Effective leaders know that when the inner core of a person (themselves) is positive, prepared, and trustworthy, the steady state of the organization is easier to maintain.

"...the most effective teaching comes from both the head and the heart..."

- Father Val Peter

Effective fearless leaders work from the head and the heart.

They have a plan that gives their leadership structure and substance. This competence is the 'head.'

Effective leaders know that there also must be warmth and sincerity that enables them to build relationships. This is the 'heart' – the compassion that creates a natural and caring connection among individuals.

"Leading without competence is pure sentimentality. Leading without compassion is pure manipulation."

- Father Val Peter

No one needs
to walk alone.

Effective fearless leaders coach others to know that there is a time to work alone and a time to ask for help.

This leaves the door open for people to think and work independently, but also promotes collaboration and team building.

When everyone in the organization has the time to personally reflect and plan and also knows that others in the organization are there for them, no one member carries the load and all members experience organizational successes.

Aim high,
but appreciate moderate.

Effective fearless leaders reach to the sky to achieve lofty goals on each and every mission.

But, they also remain realistic and make sure that they set reachable goals.

Effective leaders promote but also restrain celebrations when goals are achieved. They then move on quickly to the next objective.

They are wise to maintain superior landing gear in case there is a need to return to earth and retool during a mission.

Reprimand is an active consequence that follows an unconstructive behavior.

Effective fearless leaders know that reprimand is sometimes a must, and is used to decrease or eliminate the existence or frequency of a specific unconstructive behavior.

They know that negative behavior cannot just be ignored or hoped away.

Effective leaders think about and then act upon negative behavior knowing that if they do not take action, it is a sign of their weakness that will be recognized by members of the organization and weaken it.

Preparation is key.

Effective fearless leaders know that preparation is key before entering into any activity or task. They know that they must maintain a sense of:

1. Clarity – Have a vivid image of what is intended, even if the final product is not completely defined.
   - Why?
   - What is the target?
   - What is the path?
2. Commitment – Be free of doubt, hesitation, or second-guessing.
3. Composure – Be at ease, calm, focused, and poised.

Effective leaders know that the ability to display and reinforce these traits builds confidence in the members of the organization as they proceed through each activity or task.

Avoid ridicule,
in public or private.

Effective fearless leaders help others save face at all times and in every challenging situation. They do so by spending a great deal of time away from behind their desks and being out and about in the organization.

They observe everyone often and look for the good that each person brings to the table every day.

They understand that every situation is not 'black or white,' that there are many shades of gray, and that everything is not always what it seems to be.

Effective leaders keep their emotions and personal views in check, and take in all relevant information to make objective observations and decisions.

Their goal is to be continually working toward and maintaining organizational 'steady-state.'

Some of the greatest leaders are also the best coaches and teachers.

Effective fearless leaders know that great teachers, like excellent coaches, are able to break large amounts of information into small logical steps to reach ultimate goals.

The most effective leaders are good teachers and coaches, not just managers and bosses.

Effective leaders understand the big picture, the interconnected roles of the members of their organization, and the step-by-step procedures each division of their organization must maintain to perform at their optimal level. With this understanding, they can help everyone learn and grow into their roles and responsibilities.

Work to be a 'guide on their side,' not a 'sage on your stage.'

Effective fearless leaders facilitate. They know that they do not have to direct everything.

The more the members of an organization know about, understand, own, and are responsible for within that organization, the stronger that organization becomes.

Effective leaders understand the power of numbers. They are aware of the advantages available to the organization if all of the individuals involved feel respected and are responsible for the successes and achievements of the organization.

Every individual should feel that they are an integral part of the organization.

Effective fearless leaders periodically take a close look at, and review, the arrangement of their workplace. They make sure that each member of the organization understands that they are an integral part of the organization. Without each person's best effort, a spoke of the organizational wheel would be missing, weakening the effectiveness of the group.

They do this by observing and reviewing all aspects and procedures of the organization on a timely basis. They schedule these observations on their calendars; then they assess what has been observed.

Effective leaders are not afraid to use another person's vision or other senses to help in these assessments, and they are not fearful of another person's findings.

Reinforcers are
highly individualistic.

Principles of Fearless Leaders

Effective fearless leaders know that they must observe (stop, look, and listen to) everyone as often as possible, as each person performs the tasks of their role in their work environment. They must schedule these unannounced visits on their calendars.

They know everyone in their charge well enough to understand what each member needs or desires. There is not just one common thing (need or desire) that can be assumed for every member of the organization.

Effective leaders might just ask individuals, "What do you need, or what motivates you?"

They know that everyone must be treated as an individual; therefore 'fair' is what each person needs, and is not always the same for all.

Be proactive whenever and wherever possible … but in difficult times, act with grace.

Principles of Fearless Leaders

Effective fearless leaders think ahead. They prepare the members of their organizations by sharing how the members are expected to conduct themselves and interact with others, especially in times of difficulty.

They discuss the 'what ifs,' the scenarios that could occur ... and what to do if the 'what ifs' present themselves.

When a negative situation does take place, effective leaders help the members of the organization deal with it by coaching them through the crisis. They also emphasize how to avoid such situations in the future.

They never bring attention to any one individual in light of any negative circumstance. They stress team, team, team.

"Is it work or not?"

- George Halas,
Chicago Bears
Football Coach

Principles of Fearless Leaders

Effective fearless leaders know that their responsibilities are only work if they would rather be somewhere else.

The term 'work' is too often associated with labor and toil. The position in which a person is gainfully employed should be where they want to be because it invigorates, challenges, or brings joy. If they 'go to work' every day, they should consider looking for another way to earn a living.

Effective leaders know that they have to make a living, so they make the most of where they are right now by focusing on all the positives.

No positives? Move on.

Be an 'enthusiasticator,' as enthusiasm has an effect that is infectious.

Effective fearless leaders are enthusiastic about everything that is their organization and the goals of their organization.

They encourage others to jump right in and enjoy common experiences and challenges with them.

Effective leaders exude a passion for their work that is infectious. That passion is experienced by others in the organization and helps them to grow and develop into positive, productive members of the organization.

Salary, bonuses, and monetary compensation are generally only dissatisfiers.

Effective fearless leaders understand that money alone does not make staff members happy at work. They know that experiencing fulfilling days is more important.

Members of an organization must feel like they are needed, appreciated, and heard.

Effective leaders also know that the design of the compensation package is important in that it must be seen as fair. The compensation should also be similar to others in their field. If the compensation is not as equal, the reasons why must be carefully and compassionately explained to them and not just merely stated as matter of fact.

Recognitions such as 'Person of the Month' are usually not effective forms of positive reinforcement.

Effective fearless leaders know
that the questions asked about
recognitions may include:

1. Does the award go to the best
   performer every month?
2. Are the behaviors rewarded really
   specific and identifiable?
3. Is the award something the
   individuals want?
4. Does receiving the award
   increase or maintain
   performance?

Effective leaders look to reinforce
behaviors while they are occurring.
They spend more time away from
their desks out and about the
workplace, so they can observe
activity and actions of others to
reinforce them immediately.

Get them 'hooked.'

Effective fearless leaders recognize the importance of 'hooks' or attention-getters, and learn to engage others by using them.

They link 'hooks' to learning or experiences, and make their points relevant to all who are participating and listening. They want their audiences to be able to hear and absorb all that is presented.

Effective leaders ask themselves the 'what, where, how' and most importantly 'why' for every presentation. Their goal is that the members of the organization gain pertinent knowledge needed to perform effectively. It is not about the honor of them being the presenter.

Leaders are responsible for maintaining momentum via the smooth transition of activities or group work.

Effective fearless leaders know that even though they may want to relax when directing groups (e.g., in meetings), they must not. They must control the group, as groups tend to relax and get off-task, especially at transition times.

It is human nature to want to visit and talk when members of an organization gather together, especially when they do not have enough scheduled time to visit during the normal working day.

Effective leaders know they must direct the activities of their group meetings and that they cannot relax until they can really relax, when the meetings are over.

Make purchasing decisions based on sound research and not merely price.

Effective fearless leaders understand the importance of researching quality and value.

They take the time to gather information about the needs of the organization and how and where they can get those needs met most effectively and economically.

Effective leaders move forward steadily, but they let each purchasing decision stew a bit, so that the right product and the right price will bubble to the top.

Promote continual, consistent, and ongoing training and staff development opportunities.

Effective fearless leaders make sure that in-service training is provided to everyone in the organization to help them develop skills and improve performance.

Sharing with peers is an important final component of in-service training. If not shared with others, the training is attended, but may not be internalized.

Effective leaders know that we learn and internalize best by teaching others.

In-service training must continue over time. One-shot experiences may motivate for a while, but effective leaders want long-term improvements.

"You cannot get unfamous."

- Dave Chappelle

Effective fearless leaders know that when they are an established leader, they are always identified with their organization in the eyes of those outside of the organization.

They know that they lose some of their freedom and must think in terms of their role when in public, as others may only recognize their public image.

Effective leaders learn to deal with their positions properly. They know that how they behave in public will affect the organization, positively or negatively. They know that they are role models whether they like it or not.

The leader is always in charge in the eyes of people – inside and outside of the organization.

Principles of Fearless Leaders

Effective fearless leaders communicate desired behaviors and expectations to individuals who join the organization. They reinforce those behaviors through their own actions and words in public as well as at the workplace.

Effective leaders know that when they let down their guard, become emotional, or relax too much, they are on the road to not being in charge in the eyes of others.

Savvy works,
but not by itself
for the long haul.

Effective fearless leaders understand that genuine results come from respected systematic designs of planning and follow through, not just from intuition and savvy.

Savvy and intuition are real and positive attributes, but not all effective leaders possess them.

Effective leaders know that savvy can work to solve some problems, but it does not lead to consistent success over time. Systems using proven, step-by-step processes are the most effective means to effective problem solving and organizational growth.

Key Concepts

- Be a seeker of the 'bulbs.'
- Promote freedom of expression.
- Be responsible to the persons to whom you answer.
- Dazzle them with your footwork.
- Decrease the importance of the yearly summative evaluation.
- If you fly by the seat of your pants, be prepared for rocky landings.

"Build the team, grow the company, and have fun."

- If every person you have ever led had the true option to work with you – to choose you as their leader again – would they decide to do so?
- Adapt or be prepared to fall behind and fail.
- Every person, group, division, or echelon of individuals in the workplace must respect and appreciate the work of others.
- Help others learn to organize and develop positive workplace behaviors.
- There is no place for whining in your organization, especially on your part.
- All leaders must understand how to handle the 'uns'.
- It takes a team of skilled and cooperative players to achieve a mutual goal.
- We must know each other to know each other.
- Find the balance between introducing and reinforcing the fixed set of information that everyone needs to have in order to achieve their greatest potential.
- Because I said so!
- Positive reinforcement, when well-deserved is a 'no-brainer.'

"This is the value of the teacher..."

- Criticism should be short, to the point, and clear regarding behaviors that should be improved upon or stopped.
- Measurement alone does not modify behavior.
- Negative reinforcement produces negative talk and more.
- They are only human.
- Peer reinforcement is important.
- There are no 'buts' about it.

"...be guided by your intuition..."

- Prepare others to work and live in the future, not only in the present, and definitely not in the past.
- Know how things work, not just that they work.
- Pessimists: Curse at the wind, Optimists: Hope for wind to come up, Realists: Adjust the sails
- Engage all individuals in reflective and responsive thinking.
- Listen, listen, listen ... then think ... before you respond.
- Accept responsibility for performance outcomes of others in your charge.

> **"The purpose of goal setting should be to increase opportunities for positive reinforcement."**

- Is it a motivation problem or a skill problem?
- Ineffective practices or people have a long-term negative influence on an organization.
- All people with whom you work should regularly receive proper consequences, either positive or negative.
- Use everyday action research.
- Organize to the max and plan ahead – especially when addressing your group. Being well-prepared helps you expect the unexpected.
- Solve your problems step by step.
- Leaders of complex organizations should be able to engage in more than one action or activity at a time.
- Do not wait too long before dealing with poor performance.
- Make your expectation clear.
- Be flexible so you can roll with the punches and keep yourself in a steady state.

> **"...the most effective teaching comes from both the head and the heart..."**

- No one needs to walk alone.
- Aim high, but appreciate moderate.
- Reprimand is an active consequence that follows an unconstructive behavior.
- Preparation is key.
- Avoid ridicule, in public or private.
- Some of the greatest leaders are also the best coaches and teachers.
- Work to be a 'guide on their side,' not a 'sage on your stage.'
- Every individual should feel that they are an integral part of the organization.
- Reinforcers are highly individualistic.
- Be proactive whenever and wherever possible ... but in difficult times, act with grace.

"Is it work or not?"

- Be an 'enthusiasticator,' as enthusiasm has an effect that is infectious.
- Salary, bonuses, and monetary compensation are generally only dissatisfiers.
- Recognitions such as 'Person of the Month' are usually not effective forms of positive reinforcement.
- Get them 'hooked.'
- Leaders are responsible for maintaining momentum via the smooth transition of activities or group work.
- Make purchasing decisions based on sound research and not merely price.
- Promote continual, consistent, and ongoing training and staff development opportunities.

"You cannot get unfamous."

- The leader is always in charge in the eyes of people – inside and outside of the organization.
- Savvy works, but not by itself for the long haul.

About the Authors and Illustrator

Joseph Gulino, PH. D, is Principal of the Gulinogroup, Fearless Leaders Consulting, and of St. Peter Interparish School, Jefferson City Missouri. He was the recipient of the University of San Francisco Alumni Society Outstanding Educator in Administration Award, 1999; and the National Association of Secondary School Principals Middle Level Dissertation Award, 1997.

Shari Bullard was born in Alton, Illinois. She started "doodling" at about the age of six (at least that's what her mom always said.) Mostly self-taught, she won her first competition in eighth grade with a poster contest that was held by the Illinois Department of Agriculture. Shortly after high school graduation, she married and moved to a larger city where she continued her studies with several private teachers and by taking art education classes at Joliet JR. College.

Nathan Levy is the author of more than 40 books which have sold over 300,000 copies to teachers and parents in the United States, Europe, Asia, South America, Australia and Africa. His unique Stories with Holes series continues to be proclaimed the most popular activity used in gifted, special education and regular classrooms by hundreds of educators. An extremely popular, dynamic speaker on thinking, writing and differentiation, Nathan is in high demand as a workshop leader in school and business settings. He has worked as a school principal, district supervisor, gifted coordinator, is a company president and management trainer, as well as, the father of four daughters. Nathan's ability to transfer knowledge and strategies to audiences through humorous, thought provoking stories assures that participants leave with a plethora of new ways to approach their future endeavors.

Scott Hobson is an educational consultant, speaker and author who has presented high quality workshops to educators and parents at conferences at the national, state and local levels. With over 20 years of experience in education, Mr. Hobson has served as Principal, Assistant Principal, and Master Teacher. Scott has mentored aspiring administrators, as well as trained teachers and parents in better ways to help children learn. Scott has developed unique teaching strategies that connect critical thinking, writing and the love of learning all for the purpose of enhancing student performance and accountability. His background and experience have helped him produce five books: Breakfast for the Brain, Principles of Fearless Leadership, Affective Cognitive Thinking, Thinkology, and Miss Miller's Special Valentine.

Dynamic Workshops!

Nathan Levy is a dynamic speaker who has presented teacher, parent, and student workshops from New York to China on a wide array of topics. Nathan is a veteran educator who has taught in urban, rural, and suburban schools. He share ways to effective improve teaching and learning in the classroom and at homes. In his role as school principal, Mr. Levy has modeled instructional leadership in an exemplary manner. Mr. Levy is the author of the famous logic series Stories with Holes as well as several other educational books.

The various topics for workshops which Mr. Levy presents are of great benefit to educators as well as parents. The topics focus on such areas as:

Critical Thinking	Reading
Creativity	Writing
Effective Parenting	Science
Principal Training	Differentiating Instruction
Meeting the Standards	Teaching Hard to Reach Learners
Teaching Gifted Children	

(in and out of the regular classroom)

Please contact us for more information about our workshops from Mr. Levy, or another of our many high caliber consultants.

Nathan Levy Books, LLC

18 Moorland Blvd.
Monroe Township, NJ 08831

Phone: 732-605-1643   Fax: 732-656-7822

www.storieswithholes.com